Sauces *for* Pasta!

SAUCES *for* PASTA!

■

by Kristie Trabant
with
Andrea Chesman

 THE CROSSING PRESS • FREEDOM, CA 95019

Cover illustration and design by AnneMarie Arnold
Text illustration and design by Betsy Bayley
Printed in U.S.A.

The following sauces were created by Dorothy Rankin and are gratefully acknowledged:Bolognese Sauce I, Broccoli Blue Cheese Sauce, Broccoli de Rabe and Garlic Sauce,Calamari Sauce, Double Mushroom Sauce, Fiddlehead and Ramp Sauce, Garden Sauce with Fresh Herbs, Lamb and Eggplant Sauce, Mussels with Curried Cream, Pemaquid Crabmeat Pasta Sauce, Roasted Garlic and Mushroom Sauce, and Sun-Dried Tomato Sauce. Also, the recipes for Classic Basil Pesto, Winter Kale Pesto, and Pistachio Pesto were created by Dorothy Rankin and first appeared in *Pestos! Cooking with Herb Pastes* by Dorothy Rankin (The Crossing Press, 1985).

Library of Congress Cataloging-in-Publication Data

Trabant, Kristie
    Sauces for pasta /by Kristie Trabant with Andrea Chesman.
        p. cm.
    ISBN 0-89594-404-9 — ISBN 0-89594-403-0 (pbk.)
    1. Sauces. 2. Cookery (Pasta) I. Chesman, Andrea. II. Title.
TX819.A1T73 1990
641.8'14—dc20
                                              89-77278
                                              CIP

Contents

Introduction

Pasta is a dish that pleases just about everyone—from sophisticated diners who toss their pasta with truffles and cream to deliciously messy five-year-olds who take theirs with meatballs, please.

Pasta is unique in that it combines just as readily with rare or delicate ingredients, such as smoked eel or caviar, as it does with an economical sauce of tomatoes and seasonings. By choosing the right sauce, you can make a meal fit for a king, perfect for a child's birthday party, or fast and delicious for a hungry working person. You can make pasta a first course, side dish, or main event.

Most pasta sauces can be made in comparatively little time. While some sauces can be whipped up in less time than it takes to bring a pot of water to a boil, even the ones that must cook slowly require comparatively little actual preparation time. While the sauce slowly simmers, you can be off doing other things.

Pasta is not only versatile, universally appealing, time-saving, and (sometimes) economical, it has the added virtue of being good for you. Pasta, along with bread, cereals, and vegetables, is a complex carbohydrate (as opposed to a simple carbohydrate, which is how sugar and other refined foods are categorized). Complex carbohydrates take longer to digest than simple carbohydrates so they are very satisfying to eat—you need to eat less to feel full. A diet rich in complex carbohydrates is usually low in fats, provides sufficient protein, and ample vitamins and minerals. It is the sort of diet that fuels marathon runners and satisfies dieters (with the right sauces); it is a good choice no matter what your special dietary needs are.

Is it possible to become bored eating pasta? We don't think so. There are literally dozens of pasta shapes to choose from, not to mention as many sauces as the imagination can dream up. In this book, we have provided enough recipes to make for happy pasta eating every day for more than three months, with no repeated meals.

About Tomatoes

Canned vs. Fresh Tomatoes. Tomatoes are the basis of some wonderful sauces. The taste of a fresh tomato is so special that combined with a few herbs and scarcely cooked it can become the perfect foil for a light meal of linguine. Or it can be simmered with meat and wine and slowly cooked for hours to become a hearty soul-satisfying sauce for spaghetti.

On the other hand, the taste of an unripened tomato is dull and lifeless, and it won't spark even the finest fresh pasta. If you can't get fresh, vine-ripened tomatoes for your sauces, use canned tomatoes. These tomatoes are ripened before they are canned, so the flavor is rich and intense. Canned tomatoes, already peeled and seeded, can't be beaten for convenience, either.

Peeling and Seeding Tomatoes. If you have fresh tomatoes, you will want them peeled and seeded for some recipes. This is easy to do. Just plunge the whole tomato in boiling water for 15 to 30 seconds. Remove to a bowl of ice water or run under cold tap water. The skin can then be easily peeled away with a paring knife.

To seed a tomato, cut it in half and gently squeeze out the seeds. You can use a teaspoon to help finish the job.

Sun-Dried Tomatoes. The flavor of sun-dried tomatoes is richly intense. Combined with cream, it makes one of the most exquisite sauces for pasta.

During the drying process, the natural sweetness and flavor of the ripe tomatoes are intensified. Then the tomatoes are usually packed with herbs and olive oil. The result is plump, ready-to-use tomatoes. Just 2 tablespoons of chopped sun-dried tomatoes can transform a pleasant sauce into something quite special. The oil in which the tomatoes are packed is also very flavorful and can be used in vegetable sautés and salad dressings.

You can buy sun-dried tomatoes in specialty food stores and through mail order food companies. Be sure to buy the ones that are packed in oil. Often the loose dried tomatoes are tough and salty as a result of overdrying and the use of excess salt in the process.

If you grow your own tomatoes, you may find it is well worth the effort to make your own dried Italian plum tomatoes in a food dryer or oven. If you live in a dry, sunny climate, you can dry the tomatoes in the sun, as you dry other fruits.

To dry tomatoes, select perfect ripe Italian plum tomatoes. Slice each tomato almost in half vertically and open like a book. Remove the stem end with a small V cut and cut off any blemishes. Place the open tomatoes skin side down on drying racks or nonaluminum baking sheets. Salt them lightly; this helps to draw out the moisture.

To dry in a food dryer, set the drying racks in the food dryer about 2½ inches apart. Set on high heat and dry for 10 to 16 hours, until the tomato halves are leathery but not dry or hard. Small tomatoes will dry more quickly than large ones. Check the dryer at intervals and remove the individual tomatoes as they reach the leathery stage.

To dry in the oven, preheat the oven to 200° F. Place the baking sheets in the oven, prop open the door with a wooden spoon, and bake for 6 to 7 hours. If you have the sheets on different racks, rotate the sheets after a few hours. Remove the smaller tomatoes as they dry.

Cool the dry tomatoes slightly. Fold the tomato halves closed. Pack very tightly in half-pint jars, inserting sprigs of fresh herbs (basil, oregano, and thyme are good) or slivers of fresh garlic between the tomatoes. You can pack the tomatoes upright and make 2 layers of tomatoes with herbs in each layer. Add olive oil to completely cover the tomatoes.

A faster way to pack the jars is to start with the tomatoes completely sliced in halves. Then place a few sprigs of herbs or cloves of garlic in the bottom of half-pint or pint jars and just pack in the tomatoes and cover with olive oil.

Poke a knife in and around the edge of the jar to let any air bubbles escape. Seal the jars tightly. Store at room temperature; they are ready to use immediately.

The tomatoes will keep for months. You can pour off the oil to use in cooking and add fresh oil as needed. Use high-quality extra-virgin olive oil for the best flavor.

About Cheese

Freshly grated Parmesan cheese is an ingredient in several sauces, and it is often served at the table for sprinkling over pasta.

In these days of convenience foods, Parmesan cheese is one of the few foods that has changed little since it was first made.

In Italy, Parmesan cheese is still produced in small factories from local cow milk by a method that has remained unchanged for centuries. The finished cheese, generally aged for over a year, is hard, straw colored, slightly crumbly, mellow, and salty.

A similar cheese, made from sheep's milk and aged for about 8 months, is Pecorino Romano. The flavor of Pecorino is somewhat more robust than that of Parmesan. You can substitute Parmesan for Pecorino romano, but it is probably not a good idea to substitute Pecorino for Parmesan.

Don't buy grated cheese; it won't have the same rich flavor.

Wrapped in foil, the hard cheese keeps well in the refrigerator for several months. Freshly grated cheese can be stored in an airtight container in the freezer for up to 6 weeks without any loss of flavor. A food processor fitted with a steel blade does a good job of grating the cheese.

Choosing the Right Pasta For Your Sauce

Matching a pasta shape with a sauce is not as complicated as choosing a wine. You can, of course, combine any shape pasta with any sauce and the flavor will be just fine. But, if you have a heavy sauce, especially one that has meat in it, you will probably find that a pasta that can catch the sauce in its twists and curls, such as fusilli or small shells (conchiglie), will give you the most pleasing combination. Short, tubular pasta shapes, such as rigatoni and penne, are also good choices for heavy sauces.

A slippery oil-based sauce works well with long, thin pasta, such as cappellini or vermicelli. The oil will keep each strand separate.

Tomato, cheese, and cream-based sauces combine well with the long, thick pasta shapes, such as linguine or spaghetti, and medium-length tubular pastas, such as penne, rigatoni, and ziti.

But do experiment with the various pasta shapes and find your own favorite combinations.

Fresh versus Dried Pasta. The recent proliferation of fresh pasta shops all over the country has been made pasta eating extra pleasurable. But don't assume that fresh pasta is always better than dried pasta. There are some excellent dried pastas available—in all sorts of shapes. With fresh pasta, you are generally limited to fettuccine, linguine, or fusilli.

When shopping for a dried pasta, look for one made of durum wheat flour if it is a domestic brand. If the pasta is an Italian import, it should contain pure semolina flour.

Pasta Cooking Tips

Whether you use fresh or dried pasta, whether it is long spaghetti strands or tightly curled fusilli, you will want your pasta cooked just *al dente* (to the tooth), and not overcooked and mushy.

Cook the pasta in a tall pot with plenty of boiling water, at least 4 quarts of water to a pound of pasta. Add a little salt for flavor and a little olive oil to prevent the pasta from sticking together. Fresh pasta cooks in 15 seconds to 3 minutes, depending on its shape and thickness. Dry pasta will take from 2 minutes to 10 minutes, again depending on its shape and thickness.

Besides watching the time carefully and tasting the pasta from time to time, an easy way to guarantee properly cooked pasta is to use a large pot with a colander insert. With the colander insert, you can lift the pasta out of the boiling water at the proper instant.

Drain the pasta and serve it immediately.

Only if the pasta is going to be held before serving (not the best practice, but sometimes inevitable) should you rinse it. Use lukewarm water and toss the pasta with a little olive oil to keep the strands separate.

1
The Classics

Bolognese Sauce

Perhaps the most famous of Italian meat sauces, Bolognese Sauce is a rich one, containing meat, onions, carrots, and butter. It is a sauce that improves with age; so if you have the time, make it a day ahead.

Although traditionally made with veal and pork, we have adapted this classic to use lean ground beef and pork.

2 tablespoons olive oil
2 tablespoons butter
1 large garlic clove, minced
½ cup chopped onion
½ cup chopped celery, including some leaves
½ cup finely diced carrots
½ to ¾ pound lean ground beef and pork, or lean ground beef
⅛ teaspoon nutmeg

1½ to 2 teaspoons oregano
Salt and freshly ground pepper
½ cup dry white wine
½ cup half-and-half
1 (28-ounce) can Italian plum tomatoes, chopped (reserve and use the juice), or crushed tomatoes
½-inch by 1-inch strip lemon peel (no white pith)

Yield: 3 to 4 servings

Heat the oil and butter in a large, heavy bottomed pan. Add the garlic, onion, celery, and carrots. Sauté until the vegetables are softened, about 5 minutes. Add the ground beef and pork, nutmeg, oregano, and salt and pepper to taste. Sauté, breaking up the meat and stirring frequently, just until the meat is barely cooked and not at all browned, about 2 minutes. Add the wine. Raise the heat to medium high and cook, stirring often, until the wine evaporates, 8 to 10 minutes. Add the cream. Reduce the heat and cook gently, stirring frequently, until the cream has almost entirely reduced. Then add the tomatoes with their juice and the lemon peel.

Cover and simmer gently, stirring occasionally, until the sauce has thickened, about 2 hours. Or bake in a 325° F. oven in a covered earthenware casserole until the sauce thickens, 1½ to 2 hours.

Remove the lemon peel. Taste and correct the seasonings. Serve over hot pasta; it is recommended for all shapes and is the classic sauce for baked lasagna.

Bolognese Ragù

Ragù comes from the French word, ragoût, *which means stew. And this sauce, with its blend of onions, carrots, celery, tomatoes, and beef, is almost hearty enough to be called a stew.*

3 pounds ground beef
¼ cup olive oil
2 cups chopped onions
3 small carrots, finely chopped
1 stalk celery with leaves, finely chopped
8 garlic cloves, minced
2 (28-ounce) cans Italian plum tomatoes, chopped (reserve and use the juice), or crushed tomatoes
1 cup beef stock
1 cup dry red wine
16 fresh basil leaves, chopped
2 teaspoons dried oregano
1 teaspoon dried red pepper flakes
½ cup chopped fresh parsley
Salt and pepper to taste

Yield: 2 quarts

Put the ground beef in a large, heavy pot and cook over medium-high heat until the meat is well cooked, about 10 minutes. Remove from the heat and drain off all the fat.

Add the olive oil and heat. Then add the onions, carrots, celery, and garlic and sauté for 5 minutes. Add the remaining ingredients, stirring well. Bring slowly to a boil, and then reduce the heat to a simmer. Partially cover and simmer for 2 hours.

This sauce can be served over all kinds of pasta; it is particularly good for lasagna.

Stracotto Meat Sauce

In this hearty sauce, the meat is cooked until it falls apart.

1 cup dried porcini, cep, or cèpe
   mushrooms
1 cup warm water
2 tablespoons olive oil
1½ pounds boneless lean top round
   beef, cut into 2-inch squares
1 medium-size onion, minced
1 medium-size carrot, minced
1 celery stalk, minced
3 garlic cloves, minced
2 cups dry red wine
1 tablespoon tomato paste
¼ cup chopped fresh parsley
1 teaspoon freshly ground black pepper

Yield: 4 servings

Soak the dried mushrooms in the warm water for 30 minutes. Remove from the liquid and chop. Strain the liquid and set aside.

Heat the oil in a medium-size saucepan over medium-high heat. Add the beef and sauté until the meat is lightly browned, about 5 minutes. Reduce the heat to medium and add the onion, carrot, celery, and garlic. Sauté for 3 to 5 minutes. Add the mushrooms and soaking liquid, wine, tomato paste, parsley, and pepper. Stir until well blended. Cover tightly and simmer over very low heat for 4 hours, stirring occasionally. Add more wine or water as needed. The meat should fall apart when you are ready to serve. Serve over hot pasta (a short pasta, such as rotini, ziti, and penne, is recommended).

Sauce alla Puttanesca

The literal translation of "alla puttanesca" is "as a prostitute would prepare." But what does that tell you about the dish? It is spicy and flavorful with red peppers and capers. In some versions, a chili pepper is used instead of the red pepper flakes. In any version of this Neapolitan classic, the seasoning is bold and dramatic.

2 tablespoons olive oil
3 large garlic cloves, minced
4 cups peeled, chopped fresh Italian plum tomatoes or 1 (28-ounce) can Italian plum tomatoes, coarsely chopped (reserve and use the juice)
¼ cup chopped fresh Italian parsley
2 tablespoons finely chopped fresh basil or 1 tablespoon dried
1 teaspoon dried oregano
¼ teaspoon red pepper flakes
3 tablespoons bottled capers, well drained
1 cup pitted and halved oil-cured black olives (about 25)

Yield: 4 to 6 servings

Heat the oil in a large saucepan over medium heat. Add the garlic and sauté until pale gold, 3 to 5 minutes. Add the tomatoes and cook uncovered, stirring frequently, until slightly thickened, about 10 minutes. Add the parsley, basil, oregano, red pepper, capers, and olives. Cook for an additional 10 minutes. Serve over hot spaghetti.

Chicken Liver Spaghetti Sauce

A Venetian classic.

2 tablespoons olive oil
2 tablespoons butter
1 pound raw chicken livers, cut into
    small pieces
3 garlic cloves, minced
¼ cup sliced scallions
5 tomatoes, peeled and chopped or 1
    (28-ounce) can Italian plum tomatoes,
    chopped (reserve and use the juice)
¼ cup chopped fresh parsley
1 cup sliced mushrooms
¼ cup dry red wine
½ teaspoon dried sage
Salt and pepper to taste

Yield: 6 servings

Heat the oil and butter in a skillet over medium heat. Add the chicken livers, garlic, and scallions. Sauté until the livers are no longer pink, 5 to 6 minutes. Add the tomatoes, parsley, mushrooms, wine, and sage. Gently simmer the sauce for about 20 minutes, or until the sauce has thickened. Season with salt and pepper. Serve over hot spaghetti and pass grated Parmesan cheese.

Marinara Sauce

One of the most basic tomato sauces, it can be varied by the addition of shellfish. It is thought to be a sauce used by fishermen, as it was quick to make, and these men had no time to fuss over their food.

¼ cup olive oil
1½ cups chopped onion
3 medium-size garlic cloves, minced
3½ pounds fresh tomatoes, peeled, seeded, and chopped
6 basil leaves, finely chopped
1 teaspoon dried oregano or 2 sprigs fresh
¼ to ½ teaspoon crushed red pepper flakes
Salt and pepper to taste

Yield: 4 to 6 servings

Heat the olive oil in a heavy saucepan over medium heat for 3 minutes. Add the onions and garlic and cook for 3 minutes. Add the remaining ingredients and cook at a slow boil for about 15 minutes, or until the sauce has reduced some and thickened. Serve over hot pasta.

Sauce Alfredo

This restaurant favorite is extremely rich. You will want to offer small portions. It can be whipped up in less than 10 minutes.

12 tablespoons butter
2 cups freshly grated Parmesan cheese
1 cup heavy cream
1 cup milk
½ cup chopped fresh parsley
Pepper to taste

Yield: 4 servings

Melt the butter in a saucepan. Stir in the cheese. Then add the cream and milk and heat through; do not boil. Just before serving, add the parsley and pepper. Serve over hot pasta (fettuccine is recommended).

White Garlic Sauce

Various healing properties have been ascribed to garlic over the years. Virgil noted that garlic gave strength to harvesters. In the Middle Ages, it was prescribed to virgins to ward off vampires. Today, herbalists regard garlic as a blood cleanser and recommend it for the prevention and treatment of colds. Use the best quality olive oil—extra virgin—for this simple sauce. Garlic lovers should extra cloves for added flavor.

¾ **cup olive oil**
3 garlic cloves, minced
1 teaspoon crushed dried red pepper flakes
½ **cup chopped fresh parsley**
½ **cup grated Parmesan cheese**
Freshly ground pepper to taste

Yield: 4 servings

Heat the oil in a skillet. Add the garlic and red pepper and sauté over medium heat until the garlic is pale gold, about 3 minutes. Remove from the heat and add the parsley.

To serve, cover hot pasta with the hot sauce. Toss with the cheese and freshly ground pepper. Serve immediately and pass additional cheese at the table.

White Clam Sauce

The taste of the sea is strong in this simple sauce. You should be able to find fresh shucked clams wherever you buy fresh fish. Canned clams make an adequate substitute.

¼ cup olive oil
2 tablespoons butter
2 garlic cloves, minced
¼ cup chopped shallots
1½ cups bottled clam juice
2 cups fresh minced clams
½ cup chopped fresh parsley

Yield: 4 servings

In a saucepan, heat the olive oil and butter over medium heat. Add the garlic and shallots and sauté until they turn pale yellow, 4 to 5 minutes. Add the clam juice and simmer for 5 minutes. Stir in the clams and parsley. Bring the sauce to a boil, then remove from the heat. Serve immediately over hot pasta (vermicelli, cappellini, or spaghetti is recommended) and pass Parmesan cheese at the table.

Anchovy Sauce

The anchovies dissolve in a sauce of olive oil, butter, and garlic. This sauce is simplicity itself, and very tasty.

¼ cup olive oil
¼ cup butter
4 garlic cloves, minced
2 anchovies, minced
⅓ cup dry white wine
¼ cup chopped fresh parsley
1 teaspoon black pepper

Yield: 4 servings

Heat the oil and butter in a saucepan over medium heat. Add the garlic and sauté until pale gold, about 3 minutes. Blend in the anchovies and wine and cook over low heat, stirring constantly, until the anchovies have dissolved into the sauce, about 10 minutes. Stir in the parsley and black pepper. Serve immediately over hot pasta (vermicelli or a thin spaghetti is recommended).

Spaghetti Capri Sauce

Capri, an island in the Bay of Naples, has a number of famous dishes, not the least of which is Spaghetti Capri.

3 tablespoons olive oil
1 cup chopped onions
2 garlic cloves, minced
1 (2-ounce) can flat anchovy fillets, drained and chopped
⅓ cup dry red wine
2 fresh tomatoes, chopped
1 cup crushed tomatoes or tomato sauce
½ teaspoon crushed red pepper flakes
Black pepper to taste
1 (6½-ounce) can white albacore tuna packed in water, drained
½ cup oil-cured black kalamata olives

Yield: 4 servings

Heat the oil in a saucepan over medium heat. Add the onions and sauté for 5 minutes, until golden. Add the garlic and anchovies and sauté for 2 minutes. Add the wine and stir until blended. Add the fresh tomatoes, crushed tomatoes, red pepper, and black pepper. Cook slowly for 10 minutes. Add the tuna and olives and heat through. Serve immediately over hot spaghetti.

Carbonara Sauce

How spaghetti carbonara got its name is something of a mystery. The word carbonara derives from carbon, meaning "coal." One guess is that the mixing bowl should be so heavily coated with black pepper that it looks like the inside of a coal cellar. This dish was popularized by allied soldiers who had their first taste of it in Rome during World War II.

Sauce

Butter
1½ teaspoons coarsely ground black pepper
2 tablespoons butter
¼ pound pancetta or Canadian bacon, cut into slivers
4 eggs
¼ cup whipping cream
Salt to taste

Pasta and Topping

1 pound spaghetti
1 cup grated Parmesan cheese

Yield: 4 servings

Generously grease a large serving bowl with butter and coat it with the black pepper.

Melt the 2 tablespoons butter in a skillet, add the pancetta, and sauté for about 2 minutes. Remove from the heat and keep warm.

In a small bowl, beat the eggs with the cream and add the salt.

To serve, cook the spaghetti until just tender. Drain and return the pasta to the pot. Add the pancetta and toss. Slowly add the egg mixture to the hot pasta, tossing continuously. Pour immediately into the pepper-coated serving bowl. Add Parmesan, mix well and serve.

Classic Basil Pesto

Pesto is one of the simplest toppings for pasta, and also among the richest. The name derives from the word pestle, as the original pesto was made in a mortar and pestle. Today the food processor has mostly replaced the pestle, and pesto can be made quickly and easily. Use only fresh basil leaves, high-quality oil, and freshly grated cheese.

2 cups fresh basil leaves
2 large garlic cloves
½ cup freshly grated Parmesan cheese
2 tablespoons freshly grated Pecorino Romano cheese
¼ cup pine nuts or walnuts
½ cup high-quality olive oil
Salt and freshly ground pepper to taste

Yield: About 1 cup (4 servings)

Combine the basil, garlic, cheeses, and nuts in a food processor or blender. Process to mix. With the machine running, slowly add the olive oil. Season with salt and freshly ground pepper and process to the desired consistency. Let stand for 5 minutes.

Thin the pesto with a few tablespoons of cream or hot pasta cooking water before tossing with hot pasta (fettuccine or linguine is recommended).

Pasta Primavera

There are many different vegetables combinations you can use for pasta primavera. Fresh seasonal vegetables will yield the tastiest results. We prefer to use no more than three different vegetables in combination, as in this spring-vegetable combination of peas, asparagus, and red pepper. Other tasty combinations include zucchini, mushrooms, and string beans; broccoli, red pepper, and snow peas; peas, yellow squash, and cherry tomatoes; and broccoli, cauliflower, and red pepper. A total of 6 to 7 cups of fresh vegetables will feed 4 generously.

2 cups fresh shelled peas (approximately 1½ pounds peas in pod)
10 fresh asparagus spears, cut in 1½-inch lengths
2 cups sweet red pepper in 2-inch strips

½ cup butter
1¼ cups all-purpose cream
½ cup grated Parmesan cheese
2 tablespoons olive oil
⅓ cup pine nuts
1 garlic clove, chopped
¼ cup chopped fresh Italian parsley
Salt and freshly ground pepper to taste

Yield: 4 servings

Blanch each vegetable separately in boiling salted water for 2 to 3 minutes, until just barely tender. Drain and rinse under cold running water to halt the cooking process. This step can be done 4 to 6 hours before you are ready to serve. Store the blanched vegetables in a covered container in the refrigerator. (*Note:* If you are substituting cherry tomatoes or mushrooms for the vegetables above, do not blanch. Instead, sauté in a little olive oil with a minced garlic clove. Cook tomatoes until soft; they should still retain their shape. Cook mushrooms for about 3 minutes.)

Melt the butter in a large saucepan. Stir in the cream and Parmesan cheese. Cook over low heat until the cheese is melted. Keep warm.

Heat the olive oil in a large skillet. Add the pine nuts and cook over medium-low heat until pale gold. Add the garlic, blanched vegetables, and parsley. Stir gently until the vegetables are heated through, 3 to 5 minutes. Remove from the heat and keep warm in a large bowl.

To serve, pour the warm cream sauce over hot pasta (spaghetti or fusilli is recommended) and toss thoroughly. (If the sauce is too thick, thin with additional cream.) Add one-third of the vegetables to the pasta and toss again. Season with salt and pepper. Divide the pasta among 4 heated plates and spoon the remaining vegetables over each serving. Serve at once.

2
More Red Sauces

Sugo di Pomodoro

Sugo, *translated from the Italian, means gravy, juice, or strength. This gravy of tomatoes is a rich, full-bodied sauce that makes a good base for any lasagna, ravioli, or baked pasta dish. I make it up in large quantities and freeze the extra. A food processor makes quick work of all the minced vegetables.*

⅓ cup olive oil
3 medium-size onions, minced
3 carrots, minced
3 celery stalks, minced
4 large garlic cloves, minced
1 cup minced fresh parsley
1 (28-ounce) can Italian plum tomatoes, including the juice
2 (28-ounce) cans crushed tomatoes
1 (28-ounce) can tomato sauce
¼ cup dry red wine

2 teaspoons dried oregano or 2 tablespoons fresh
2 teaspoons dried marjoram or 2 tablespoons fresh
4 teaspoons dried basil or ¼ cup chopped fresh
1 teaspoon freshly ground black pepper

Yield: 4 quarts

In a large kettle, heat the oil over medium heat. Add the onions, carrots, celery, garlic, and parsley. Cook, stirring occasionally, for 15 minutes. Break up the Italian plum tomatoes and add along with the crushed tomatoes and tomato sauce. Then add the wine, dried herbs, and pepper. (If you are using fresh herbs, add during the last half hour of cooking.) Reduce the heat to low and cook, uncovered, for about

1 hour. Stir occasionally to prevent scorching. Serve over hot pasta or use in a baked pasta dish.

Fresh Tomato Butter Sauce

3 tablespoons butter
3 cups peeled, seeded, and chopped
   fresh tomatoes
6 basil leaves, chopped
Salt and pepper to taste
2 tablespoons chopped fresh parsley
Parmesan cheese

Yield: 4 servings

Melt the butter in a skillet over medium-heat. Add the tomatoes, basil, and salt and pepper. Increase the heat and cook until the sauce begins to boil. Then reduce the heat to a simmer and cook for about 20 minutes, or until the juice has cooked away a bit.

Serve over the hot pasta and sprinkle with grated Parmesan cheese.

Tomato Zucchini Sauce

The combination of fresh tomatoes, zucchini, and basil make this the perfect sauce for a light summer meal.

2 medium-size zucchini (about 1 pound)
1½ pounds ripe tomatoes (4 to 5 medium-size tomatoes)
6 tablespoons olive oil
3 medium-size garlic cloves, crushed
½ teaspoon crushed dried red pepper flakes
¼ cup chopped fresh basil
20 small pitted black olives (preferably imported olives)
Salt and freshly ground black pepper to taste

Yield: 4 to 6 servings

Trim the ends from the zucchini. Cut each zucchini crosswise into 2-inch slices. Cut each slice into sixths. You should have about 3½ cups.

Remove the cores from the tomatoes and cut into ½-inch cubes.

Heat 4 tablespoons of the olive oil in a large skillet over medium heat. Add the zucchini and sauté just until the zucchini is tender, 3 to 5 minutes. Remove from the skillet and set aside. Add the remaining 2 tablespoons olive oil to the skillet. Then add the garlic and sauté briefly. Add the tomatoes and cook, stirring often, for 5 minutes. Add the hot pepper, basil, black olives, and zucchini. Simmer for 10 minutes. Season with salt and pepper.

Serve over hot pasta (fusilli is recommended) and pass grated Parmesan cheese on the side.

Chicken Cacciatora Sauce

Cacciatora sauce, "hunter's style," is a rich sauce of tomatoes, mushrooms, herbs, and wine.

¼ cup olive oil
2 large boned chicken breasts, cut into bite-size pieces
3 garlic cloves, minced
2 medium-sized onions, chopped
2 cups sliced fresh mushrooms
1 (28-ounce) can Italian-style plum tomatoes, including the juice
1 large green pepper, thinly sliced
¼ cup chopped fresh parsley
1 teaspoon dried oregano
½ teaspoon dried thyme
1 bay leaf
⅔ cup dry red wine

Yield: 6 to 8 servings

Heat the oil in a large skillet over medium high heat. Add the chicken and sauté until lightly brown, 5 to 8 minutes. Remove the pieces to a plate with a slotted spoon. Add the garlic and onion and sauté in the pan drippings over medium heat for 3 minutes. Add the mushrooms and sauté for 5 minutes. Add the tomatoes, green pepper, parsley, oregano, thyme, bay leaf, wine, and chicken. Simmer gently for 25 to 30 minutes. Serve over hot spaghetti.

Tomato, Ham, and Vodka Sauce

The vodka gives the sauce a sharp bite, which contrasts nicely with the salty ham. Do use a good quality vodka.

4 tablespoons butter
1 onion, chopped
¼ pound cooked ham, finely chopped
1 cup canned crushed tomatoes
½ cup vodka
1 cup heavy cream or half-and-half
3 dashes Tabasco sauce

Yield: 4 servings

Melt the butter in a skillet over medium heat. Add the onions and sauté until soft, about 3 minutes. Add the ham, tomatoes, and vodka and simmer until the sauce has reduced by about one-fourth, 10 to 15 minutes. Slowly add the cream and Tabasco. Stir until well blended and hot. Serve over hot pasta (penne or farfelle is recommended).

Lamb and Eggplant Sauce

You can substitute beef or pork if lamb is unavailable.

2 tablespoons olive oil
1 tablespoon butter
1 cup chopped onions
1 garlic clove, minced
3 cups peeled and cubed eggplant (½-inch cubes)
½ teaspoon crumbled dried rosemary
1 teaspoon dried oregano
½ cup red wine
¾ cup lean ground lamb
1 cup diced mushrooms (¼-inch dices)
Salt and freshly ground pepper to taste
1½ cups peeled and chopped ripe tomatoes or drained, cubed, canned Italian tomatoes
½ cup tomato juice

2 tablespoons tomato paste
2 tablespoons chopped fresh parsley

Yield: 4 servings

Heat the olive oil and butter in a large skillet. Add the onions and garlic and sauté for 2 minutes. Add the eggplant, rosemary, and oregano, and continue to sauté, adding a few tablespoons of wine as you cook, until the eggplant has softened, 5 to 8 minutes. Remove from the skillet to a large bowl and set aside.

Divide the lamb into 2 batches. Sauté each batch in the skillet over medium-high heat briefly, just until the pink color disappears. Remove from the skillet with a slotted spoon and add to the eggplant. Add the mushrooms and salt and pepper to the skillet and sauté for about 2 minutes.

In a deep saucepan, combine the eggplant and lamb mixture with the mushrooms and the remaining wine, tomatoes, tomato juice, tomato paste, and parsley. Simmer for 20 to 30 minutes, until the lamb is tender.

Serve over hot pasta (fusilli is recommended). If the sauce is too thick, add approximately ¼ cup of the pasta cooking water to the sauce before pouring over the pasta.

3
More Cream Sauces

Light Cheese Sauce

Made with low-fat cottage cheese and ricotta cheese, this is a guilt-free cheese sauce. I like to combine the sauce with lightly blanched fresh asparagus (1 pound will do for 4 to 6 servings) and linguine.

1 garlic clove
1 cup low-fat cottage cheese
1 cup low-fat ricotta cheese
¼ cup grated Parmesan cheese
¼ cup dry white wine
2 tablespoons minced fresh parsley

Yield: 4 to 6 servings

Mince the garlic in a food processor. Add the cottage and ricotta cheeses and process until smooth and creamy. Pour into a medium-size saucepan and gently heat over medium-low heat, stirring frequently for 5 to 8 minutes, or until the sauce is hot, but not bubbling. Add the Parmesan cheese, wine, and parsley, stirring until the sauce is well blended and hot. Do not overcook. Serve hot over hot pasta.

Fontina Cheese Sauce

Made in the Piedmont area of Italy, fontina cheese is a fat, semi-soft, rich cheese that is prized for its smooth melting qualities. The sweetly nutty, mellow flavor of Fontina is said to come from its aging process, which takes place in well-aired stone buildings at elevations of 10,000 feet.

3 tablespoons olive oil
2 tablespoons minced shallots
¼ cup flour
2 cups milk
2½ cups grated fontina cheese
3 tablespoons Marsala wine
½ teaspoon white pepper
Dash cayenne pepper

Yield: 4 servings

Heat the oil in a saucepan over medium heat. Add the shallots and sauté for 3 minutes. Sprinkle the flour into the saucepan, stirring until it is well blended. Slowly whisk in the milk and continue to cook and stir until the sauce has thickened. Reduce the heat to low and add the cheese and wine. Stir until the cheese melts. Add the white pepper and cayenne. Serve immediately over hot pasta. Do not overcook.

Brie and Green Chile Sauce

This unusual combination of ingredients makes an exquisitely flavorful sauce. The cheese melts rather quickly, but it must be vigorously whisked into the sauce to blend well.

1 tablespoon butter
1 tablespoon minced shallots
1 garlic clove, minced
½ cup chicken stock or broth
1 cup whipping cream or half-and-half
½ cup dry white wine
¼ teaspoon chili powder
½ pound brie, rind discarded and re-
    maining cheese diced (½-inch pieces)
1 (7½-ounce) can whole chili peppers
    (mild or hot), sliced into small strips

Yield: 4 to 6 servings

Melt the butter over moderate heat in a large skillet. Add the shallots and sauté until soft, about 3 minutes. Add the garlic and sauté for 1 minute. Add the chicken stock, cream, wine, and chili powder. Bring to a boil. Then reduce the heat and simmer, stirring occasionally, for 15 to 20 minutes, or until the sauce is reduced by almost half. Whisk in the brie a little at a time until the brie has melted. Add the chili peppers. Serve at once over hot pasta (fettuccine is recommended).

Mushroom Cheese Sauce

This is a simple, elegant sauce. It is wonderful on spinach fettuccine.

¼ cup butter
2 tablespoons olive oil
½ pound fresh mushrooms, sliced
2 tablespoons all-purpose flour
1 cup milk
¾ cup light cream
¼ cup dry white wine
1 cup grated Parmesan cheese
Salt and pepper to taste

Yield: 4 servings

Heat the butter and oil in a skillet over medium heat. Add the mushrooms and sauté until tender, about 5 minutes. Sprinkle the flour over the mushrooms and blend it in. Slowly add the milk and cream, stirring continuously, and cook until the mixture becomes thick and bubbly. Reduce the heat to a simmer and stir in the wine and cheese. Season with salt and pepper. Serve at once over hot pasta. Pass additional Parmesan cheese at the table.

Roasted Garlic and Mushroom Sauce

Although the amount of garlic may seem excessive—even for garlic lovers—the flavor of this sauce is surprisingly subtle. Roasting the garlic mellows its flavor, which is nicely complemented by the mushrooms.

2 garlic bulbs
3 tablespoons butter
¼ cup chopped shallots
3 to 4 cups chopped mushrooms
1 cup chicken stock or broth
1 teaspoon dried thyme
½ teaspoon crushed dried red pepper flakes
2 bay leaves
1 cup light cream
⅔ cup grated Gruyère cheese
Salt to taste

Yield: 3 to 4 servings

To roast the garlic, preheat the oven to 375° F. Wrap the garlic, whole, in a folded packet of heavy-duty aluminum foil. Roast in the preheated oven for 1¼ hours. Or, slice off the top of the bulb, place the bulb in a 1-quart glass measuring cup, add ¼ cup of the chicken stock, cover tightly with microwave plastic wrap, and microwave at 100 percent power (700 watts) for 5 minutes. Remove from the microwave, prick the plastic wrap to release the steam, and let stand, covered, for 10 minutes.

In a large skillet, melt the butter. Add the shallots and mushrooms and sauté until the butter has been absorbed, about 3 minutes. Add the chicken stock, thyme, red pepper, and bay leaves. Simmer over low heat, stirring frequently, until the liquid has reduced by half, 3 to 4 minutes.

With your fingers, squeeze the garlic puree from each clove into a small bowl. Mash, then whip the puree with a fork. Add to the sauce. Simmer for just 1 minute. Remove the bay leaves. Add the cream and cheese. Simmer, stirring frequently, for 2 minutes. Season with salt. Serve over hot pasta (cappellini or fettuccine is recommended).

Four Mushroom Wine Sauce

Until recently, cultivated white mushrooms were the only mushrooms one could find without an extensive search. Today dried black mushrooms and shitakes are found wherever Chinese foods are sold, and that includes some supermarkets. Porcini (also known as ceps or cèpes) are most likely found in gourmet food shops. Although dried mushrooms are expensive, a little goes a long way, and they add an incredible amount of flavor.

⅓ cup dried shitake mushrooms
⅓ cup dried black mushrooms
⅓ cup porcini mushrooms
1 cup boiling water
3 tablespoons butter
8 medium-size white cultivated
   mushrooms, sliced
1 cup chicken stock or broth
½ cup dry white wine
¼ cup sliced scallions with green tops
1 small garlic clove, minced
1¾ cups whipping cream or half-and-half
1 tablespoon lemon juice
Salt and freshly ground pepper to taste

Yield: 4 to 6 servings

Combine the dried mushrooms and boiling water in a bowl. Set aside for 30 minutes.

Melt the butter in a sauté pan over medium heat. Add the sliced white mushrooms and sauté until the mushrooms have released their moisture, about 5 minutes. Set aside.

Combine the chicken stock, wine, scallions, and garlic in a saucepan and bring to a boil. Boil until the mixture is reduced to about ¾ cup.

Drain the dried mushrooms and add the

soaking liquid to the reduced chicken stock. Slice the mushrooms and add to the sauce along with the sautéed white mushrooms and cream. Bring to a slow boil and continue to boil, stirring frequently, until the sauce has reduced and thickened slightly. Add the lemon juice. Season with salt and pepper. Serve over hot pasta (fusilli is recommended).

Double Mushroom Sauce

Fresh shitake mushrooms are best in this sauce, but dried shitakes are certainly good substitutes.

2 tablespoons butter
2 tablespoons vegetable oil
½ cup chopped shallots
2 cups sliced fresh shitake mushrooms, or 1⅓ cups dried shitakes, soaked in warm water for 1 hour, then sliced
2 cups sliced cultivated mushrooms
¼ cup dry white wine
¼ teaspoon dried thyme
Salt and freshly ground pepper to taste
6 tablespoons julienne-sliced roasted sweet red peppers (homemade or bottled)
¼ cup whipping cream
2 tablespoons grated Gruyère or Swiss-type cheese or freshly grated Parmesan cheese

Yield: 4 servings

In a medium-size skillet, heat the butter and oil. Add the shallots and sauté for 2 minutes. Add the mushrooms and sauté, stirring frequently, until the mushrooms begin to soften, 2 to 3 minutes. Add the wine, thyme, and salt and pepper. Continue sautéing until the wine begins to reduce. Add the peppers and sauté for 2 minutes. Add the cream and cheese. Taste for seasoning. Serve over hot pasta (vermicelli is recommended).

Red, Yellow, and Green Sauce

A rich, buttery sauce for people who don't count calories.

Sauce

¼ cup butter
½ cup fresh or frozen peas
1 large sweet yellow pepper, julienned
1½ cups medium or light cream
½ pound fresh plum tomatoes, peeled and diced

Pasta and Topping

¾ pound rotini, ziti, or farfelle
¼ cup butter
½ cup grated Parmesan cheese

Yield: 4 to 6 servings

Melt the ¼ cup butter in a large skillet. Add the peas and sweet peppers and sauté for about 3 minutes. Add the cream and bring to a slow boil. Cook until the sauce is reduced by about one-quarter. Add the tomatoes and cook for 10 minutes.

Cook the pasta until just *al dente*, then drain. Pour into a warmed serving bowl. Add the remaining ¼ cup butter and Parmesan cheese. Toss to mix. Pour the hot sauce over and toss again. Serve immediately.

Artichoke Hearts and Cream

Artichoke hearts packed in water are readily available in the supermarket. They are far superior to frozen artichoke hearts, which are usually mushy. Each can contains 5 to 7 hearts.

10 bacon slices
2 tablespoons butter
½ cup sliced scallions, including the green tops
½ cup whipping cream or half-and-half
½ cup grated Parmesan cheese
¼ cup minced fresh parsley
Salt and pepper to taste
2 (14-ounce) cans artichoke hearts packed in water, drained and halved
Parmesan cheese for topping

Yield: 4 to 6 servings

Fry the bacon until crisp. Drain on paper towels; set aside. When cool, crumble.

In a large skillet, melt the butter over medium heat. Add the scallions and sauté for 3 minutes. Add the cream and simmer until the sauce thickens slightly. Add ½ cup Parmesan cheese and the parsley. Season with salt and pepper. Add the artichokes and heat through.

Pour the hot sauce over hot pasta (spaghetti is recommended). Top with the crumbled bacon and serve immediately with additional cheese.

Fiddlehead and Ramp Sauce

Fiddleheads, the tender young shoots of the wild ostrich fern, make their annual appearance in supermarkets and specialty food stores in April and May. The flavor is sometimes described as a cross between spinach and asparagus. They go very well with ramps, or wild leeks, but scallions or shallots make a fine substitute.

4 cups fresh fiddleheads
8 cups water
¼ cup butter
1 cup chopped ramps or scallions and shallots
2 cups chopped mushrooms
1 cup chicken stock or broth
½ teaspoon dried savory
⅔ cup whipping cream
3 ounces cream cheese, cubed
Salt and freshly ground pepper to taste

Yield: 4 servings

To clean the fiddleheads, bring the water to a boil in a saucepan and add the fiddleheads. Allow the water to return to a boil and boil for 1 minute. Drain and hand rinse any remaining brown fern residue from the fiddleheads. Set aside.

Heat the butter in a large skillet and add the ramps. Sauté for 2 minutes. Add the fiddleheads and mushrooms and continue to sauté until tender, 4 to 5 minutes, adding the chicken stock a few tablespoons at a time. Continue to cook until the liquid is reduced by about half.

Add the savory. Stir in the cream and cream cheese and cook gently over low heat until the cream cheese is melted. Season with salt and pepper.

Serve over hot pasta (capellini, fettuccine, or linguine is recommended).

53

4
More Seafood Sauces

Tomato Sauce with Shrimp and Feta

Tomatoes, shrimp, and feta cheese bring together the sunny flavors of the Mediterranean. If you start with frozen cleaned shrimp, this sauce takes very little time to prepare.

4 tablespoons olive oil
1 tablespoon minced garlic
2 cups peeled, seeded, and chopped ripe tomatoes
⅓ cup dry white wine
¼ cup chopped fresh basil
1 teaspoon dried oregano
Salt and freshly ground pepper to taste
30 medium shrimp
⅛ teaspoon crushed dried red pepper flakes
½ pound feta cheese, crumbled

Yield: 4 to 6 servings

Heat 2 tablespoons of the oil in a saucepan over medium heat, add the garlic, and sauté for about 1 minute. Add the tomatoes and cook, stirring constantly, for 2 to 3 minutes. Add the wine, basil, oregano, and salt and pepper. Simmer, stirring occasionally, for about 10 minutes.

In a medium-size sauté pan, heat the remaining 2 tablespoons olive oil over high heat. Add the shrimp and sauté for 1 to 2 minutes, or until the shrimp are pink and firm. Sprinkle with the red pepper. Add to the tomato sauce and keep warm.

Serve immediately over hot pasta (rigatoni or a tubular-shaped pasta is recommended). Sprinkle each serving with the feta cheese.

Shrimp and Snow Peas Dijon

1 pound snow peas
5 tablespoons butter
⅓ cup chopped shallots
1½ pounds medium-size shrimp, peeled
  and deveined
¾ cup dry white wine
½ cup Dijon-style mustard
¾ cup heavy cream or half-and-half

Yield: 4 to 6 servings

Blanch the peas in boiling water for 2 to 3 minutes. Drain and rinse in cool water to stop the cooking. Drain again and set aside.

Melt the butter in a skillet over medium heat. Add the shallots and cook slowly for 15 minutes. Increase the heat, add the shrimp, and sauté for 2 to 3 minutes or until the shrimp are bright pink. Remove the shrimp and set aside. Pour the wine into the skillet and cook until the liquid is reduced by about two-thirds. Reduce the heat to low and whisk in the mustard. Stir in the cream and simmer for 10 to 15 minutes. Add the peas and shrimp and serve at once over hot pasta (farfelle or penne goes well).

Shrimp Creole Sauce

Shrimp Creole made with rice is a classic, but this richly flavored sauce for pasta has just the right taste of Creole cooking. I add the green pepper with the shrimp at the last minute to retain its color and crunch.

⅓ cup olive oil
1 cup chopped onions
4 garlic cloves, minced
½ cup chopped celery
½ teaspoon dried oregano
½ teaspoon white pepper
½ teaspoon cayenne
½ teaspoon paprika
½ teaspoon black pepper
½ teaspoon dried thyme
½ teaspoon dried basil
1 (1-pound) can peeled tomatoes, chopped
1 (1-pound) can unseasoned tomato sauce
White wine (optional)
1 pound small shrimp, peeled and deveined
½ cup chopped green pepper
4 scallions, including green tops, sliced
½ cup chopped fresh parsley

Yield: 4 to 6 servings

Heat the oil in a saucepan over medium heat. Add the onions, garlic, and celery and sauté for about 3 minutes. Add the seasonings, tomatoes, and tomato sauce. Cook over low heat for 20 minutes to allow the flavors to blend. If the sauce becomes too thick, thin with some white wine.

Add the shrimp, green pepper, scallions, and parsley and cook over medium heat for about 5 minutes, until the shrimp are tender. Serve over hot pasta (shells or ziti is recommended).

Golden Tomato Curry with Shrimp

There's no substitute for the yellow tomatoes in this recipe. The mild flavor of yellow tomatoes makes a perfect backdrop for the curry, and the lovely yellow sauce is exquisite over spinach fettuccine.

2 tablespoons olive oil
4 medium-size onions, chopped
2 tablespoons curry powder
½ teaspoon ground turmeric
5 medium-size yellow tomatoes, peeled
   and chopped
1 medium-size green pepper, julienned
1 medium-size sweet red pepper,
   julienned
1 pound frozen cooked shrimp, defrosted

Yield: 4 servings

Heat the oil in a medium-size skillet over medium heat. Add the onions, curry powder, and turmeric. Sauté for 5 minutes. Add the tomatoes and cook over low heat for 15 minutes. Add the peppers and shrimp. Cook over medium heat for 5 minutes, stirring occasionally. Serve over hot pasta (spinach fettuccine is recommended).

Fresh Crab and Tomato Sauce

This sauce is for those fortunate to get fresh crabmeat and garden-fresh tomatoes.

2 tablespoons olive oil
2 large garlic cloves, minced
2½ pounds fresh tomatoes, peeled, seeded, and chopped
Salt and pepper to taste
¼ cup chopped fresh parsley
1 pound fresh crabmeat, cartilage removed

Yield: 4 servings

Heat the olive oil in a skillet over medium-high heat. Add the garlic and sauté until pale gold. Add the tomatoes and season with salt and pepper. Cook the tomatoes at a slow boil for 15 to 20 minutes. Add the parsley and crabmeat and simmer for 3 minutes. Remove from the heat and serve over hot pasta (spaghetti is recommended).

Pemaquid Crabmeat Pasta Sauce

When the boats come in to New Harbor, Maine, on the Pemaquid peninsula, the fresh crabmeat goes so quickly that reservations are necessary. This recipe was created to take advantage of that sweet Maine crabmeat, which we bought at the general store.

2 tablespoons butter
2 tablespoons extra-virgin olive oil
¼ cup chopped shallots
2 teaspoons crushed dried red pepper flakes
2 tablespoons minced fresh basil or 1 tablespoon dried
3 cups peeled, chopped ripe tomatoes
2 cups fresh crabmeat, cartilage removed
⅔ cup whipping cream

2 to 3 tablespoons chopped fresh parsley
Salt to taste

Yield: 4 servings

In a medium-size sauté pan, heat the butter and oil. Add the shallots and red pepper and sauté for about 2 minutes, just until the shallots begin to soften. Add the basil and tomatoes. Sauté, stirring constantly, for 2 minutes. Add the crabmeat. Lift and gently turn with a spatula as it cooks for a minute or two. Add the cream, parsley, and salt. Serve over hot pasta.

Creamy Crab Sauce

Here's a simpler version of the Pemaquid Crabmeat Sauce. In this one, a rich Bechamel sauce is studded with crabmeat, fresh tomato bits, and scallions.

2 tablespoons butter
½ cup thinly sliced scallions
3 tablespoons flour
1 cup half-and-half
¼ cup dry white wine
½ cup chopped, seeded ripe tomatoes
1 pound cooked crabmeat, cartilage
　　removed

Yield: 4 servings

Melt the butter in a sauté pan over medium heat. Add the scallions and sauté for about 2 minutes. Blend in the flour with a wooden spoon, stirring to removing any lumps. Remove from the heat and slowly stir in the cream. Continue stirring until well blended, then return to the heat and cook until thick and bubbling. Add the wine, reduce the heat to a simmer. You may want to thin the sauce more by adding a little more wine. Add the tomatoes and crabmeat. Remove from the heat and keep warm. Serve over hot pasta (penne or conchiglie is recommended).

Tuna Wine Sauce

This zesty sauce is easy to prepare from ingredients you are likely to have stocked in the cupboard.

3 tablespoons olive oil
1 medium-size garlic clove, minced
2 scallions, including some green, thinly sliced
2 tablespoons all-purpose flour
1 cup fish or chicken stock (or bouillon)
½ cup dry white wine
1 (6½-ounce) can chunk light tuna packed in oil, drained
2 tablespoons capers, rinsed and drained
2 tablespoons lemon juice
3 dashes Tabasco sauce
Black pepper to taste

Yield: 4 servings

Heat the oil in a sauté pan over medium heat. Add the garlic and scallions and sauté for 2 minutes. Add the flour and blend well. Stir in the stock and wine, stirring constantly until thickened. Reduce the heat and stir in the tuna and capers. Add the lemon juice, Tabasco, and pepper. Serve hot over pasta.

Mussels with Tomato Sauce

The briny, sweet flavor of mussels pairs well with tomatoes.

4 pounds mussels in shell
1½ cups dry white wine
4 large garlic cloves
2 large onions, chopped
½ cup chopped fresh parsley
8 fresh basil leaves, chopped
3 tablespoons olive oil
3 large ripe tomatoes, peeled and
    chopped or 2 cups canned tomatoes,
    drained
4 dashes Tabasco sauce
2 tablespoons lemon juice
Salt and pepper to taste

Yield: 4 servings

Scrub the mussels to remove any dirt. Pull off the beards (a twisted fiber connected to the shell). Discard any mussels that are open.

In a large pot, combine the mussels, wine, 2 of the garlic cloves, 1 chopped onion, and 2 tablespoons of the parsley. Cover, bring to a boil, and steam the mussels until the shells have opened, about 5 minutes. Discard any unopened shells. Remove the mussels from the shells.

Strain the cooking liquid through a fine sieve or 2 thicknesses of rinsed cheesecloth into a saucepan. Cook over medium-high heat until the liquid has reduced to about 1 cup. Remove from the heat.

In a medium-size skillet, heat the olive oil over medium heat and add the remaining onion and garlic. Sauté until the onion is soft, about 3 minutes. Add the tomatoes, basil, remaining 2 tablespoons parsley, Tabasco, and reduced mussel liquid. Simmer the mixture for 15 minutes. Add the mussels with the Tabasco sauce, lemon juice, and salt and pepper.

Serve over hot pasta (linguine is recommended) and sprinkle with Parmesan cheese.

Mussels with Curried Cream

If you buy your curry powder at a specialty or Oriental food store, you will probably find it fresh tasting and quite hot. If you are using a supermarket brand, increase the curry powder to taste.

4 pounds mussels in shell
¾ cup dry white wine
4 tablespoons olive oil
1½ teaspoons curry powder
½ cup chopped shallots
2 cups chopped mushrooms
1½ cups chopped ripe tomatoes
¾ to 1 cup light cream
¼ cup minced fresh parsley

Yield: 4 servings

Scrub the mussels to remove any dirt. Pull off the beards (a twisted fiber connected to the shell). Discard any mussels that are open.

In a large pot, combine the mussels with the wine and 2 tablespoons of the oil. Cover, bring to a boil, and steam the mussels over high heat for 5 minutes, or until the shells have opened. Discard any unopened mussels. Remove the mussels from the shells. Strain the liquid through a fine sieve or 2 thicknesses of rinsed cheesecloth. Reserve the broth.

In a medium-size saucepan, heat the remaining 2 tablespoons olive oil. Add the curry powder and simmer over low heat, stirring constantly, for 1 minute. Add the shallots and mushrooms. Sauté, stirring constantly, until the shallots and mushrooms soften slightly. Add a little of the reserved mussel broth at intervals, stirring and allowing the liquid to reduce. When all the broth has been added, and the amount of liquid has reduced to 1 to 1½ cups, add the chopped tomatoes. Cook for 2 minutes, stirring constantly. Fold in the reserved mussels and add cream to the desired consistency.

Note: You can substitute 2 cups fresh picked mussel meat for the mussels in shell. Substitute 1 cup clam broth for the mussel broth.

Serve over hot pasta (tomato spirals or tiny seashell pasta is recommended). Toss gently, sprinkle with minced fresh parsley, and serve immediately.

Calamari Sauce

Calamari, or squid, used to be a rarity outside of stores that cater to an Italian population, but it is becoming increasingly available and inexpensive. The secret to cooking calamari is to cook it quickly; overcooked it becomes quite rubbery. This sauce cooks in about 10 minutes.

If you have never prepared a squid before, don't be daunted by this unusual looking sea creature. Simply grasp the squid with one hand, reach inside the body and pull the head and tentacles away. Pull off and discard the mottled skin. Feel inside the body for the transparent cartilage (it looks and feels like plastic); draw it out and discard it. Then wash the body inside and out under cold running water. Separate the two flaps from the body; they pull away easily. Locate the ink sac, which is attached to the head, remove, and discard it. Then cut the tentacles from the head. Cut the body into thick rings, slice the flaps into strips and cut the tentacles to an easily forked size.

2 teaspoons minced garlic
1 cup chopped onions
1 (28-ounce) can crushed plum tomatoes (3 cups)
1 teaspoon dried oregano
1 teaspoon dried basil
½ teaspoon crushed dried red pepper flakes
⅓ to ½ cup dry red wine
Salt to taste (about ½ teaspoon)
1 pound fresh squid, including tentacles
½ cup chopped fresh parsley

Yield: 4 servings

Combine the garlic, onions, tomatoes, oregano, basil, red pepper, wine, and salt in a medium-size saucepan. Simmer for 4 minutes.

Rinse the squid and slice into pieces ½ inch thick. Add the squid and the parsley to the sauce and simmer until the squid is just done, 5 to 6 minutes. Do not overcook or the squid will be rubbery in texture. Remove from the heat at once and toss with hot pasta (tricolor fusilli is recommended).

Grilled Fish and Mushroom Sauce

The rich, smoky flavor of fish grilled over a charcoal flame combines with mushrooms and wine in this delicate sauce.

The best utensil to use when grilling fillets of flaky fish is a two-sided, hinged grill with handle. Oil it well.

For the fish bouillon, you can use stock made from bones and fish heads. Otherwise, you can use fish bouillon cubes made by Knorr. Use ½ cube in 1¼ cups hot water.

1½ **pounds cod, cusk, hake, ar any firm white-fleshed fish fillets (choose thick fillets if possible)**
2 **tablespoons butter**
1 **tablespoon olive oil**
½ **cup chopped shallots**
1½ **cups sliced mushrooms**
3 **tablespoons flour**

1¼ **cups fish bouillon or water**
½ **cup dry vermouth**
2 **tablespoons chopped fresh parsley**
½ **teaspoon white pepper**

Yield: 4 to 6 servings

Grill the fish over a hot fire. The cooking time (about 3 to 5 minutes per side) will depend on how thick the fillets are. Test for doneness by pressing down with a finger. The fish should be firm to the touch and the flesh should look opaque. Set aside.

Heat the butter and oil in a large skillet over medium heat. Add the shallots and mushrooms and sauté for 5 minutes. Sprinkle the flour into the pan, stirring constantly until it is well blended. Slowly add the fish bouillon or water and stir until the sauce is smooth and thick.

Add the vermouth, parsley, and white pepper. Stir until the sauce is well blended and begins to bubble slightly. Add the fish. The fish will flake into small pieces as you gently stir it into the sauce. Heat thoroughly and serve over hot pasta (linguine is recommended).

Smoked Salmon Sauce

3 tablespoons butter
¼ cup chopped shallots
3 scallions, including some green tops, thinly sliced
1 cup finely chopped mushrooms
1 cup dry vermouth or dry white wine
1½ cups half-and-half
2 tablespoons flour
1 pound smoked salmon, cut into bite-size pieces
2 tablespoons chopped fresh dill
Salt and pepper to taste

Yield: 4 servings

Melt the butter in a medium-size skillet over medium heat. Add the shallots, scallions, and mushrooms and sauté for 3 minutes. Add ¾ cup of the vermouth or wine. Reduce the heat and slowly cook until the liquid has reduced by half. Add the half-and-half and increase the heat to medium, stirring the sauce until it is hot but not bubbling.

Make a thin paste by combining the flour with the remaining ¼ cup vermouth or wine. Slowly add to the sauce, stirring constantly, and cook until the sauce has thickened, 3 to 5 minutes. Add the salmon, dill, and salt and pepper. Stir to blend and cook for 3 minutes. Serve hot over hot pasta.

5
New Sauces

Corn and Tomato Sauce

Sweet corn and red ripe tomatoes are the quintessential vegetables of summer.

3 tablespoons olive oil
1 cup chopped onions
½ pound prosciutto (¹/₈-inch slices), cut into thin strips
2½ cups peeled, seeded, and chopped fresh tomatoes or 1 (28-ounce) can Italian plum tomatoes, drained
1 cup dry white wine
½ cup half-and-half
¼ teaspoon crushed dried red pepper flakes
2 cups fresh corn cut off the cob or 2 cups frozen or canned corn
Salt and pepper to taste

Yield: 4 to 6 servings

Heat the olive oil over medium heat in a skillet. Add the onion and cook until pale gold, about 5 minutes. Add the prosciutto along with the tomatoes, wine, half-and-half, and red pepper. Cook at a slow boil until the sauce has reduced to a creamy consistency, about 10 minutes. Add the corn and cook for another 5 minutes. Season with salt and pepper. Serve over hot pasta (penne is recommended).

Red and Yellow Tomato Sauce

Plan to make this sauce at the height of the fresh tomato season. Yellow tomatoes make a milder, less acidic tomato sauce. Of course, if you can't find yellow tomatoes, then use all red tomatoes.

5 tablespoons olive oil
6 sweet Italian sausages, casing removed and meat broken into small pieces
4 medium-size onions, chopped
4 carrots, finely chopped
3 celery ribs, finely chopped
3 garlic cloves, minced
4 large yellow tomatoes, peeled, seeded, and chopped
4 large red tomatoes, peeled, seeded, and chopped
½ cup coarsely chopped fresh basil
½ cup chopped fresh parsley
1 teaspoon crushed dried red pepper flakes
Salt and pepper to taste

Yield: 6 servings

Heat 1 tablespoon of the oil in a large saucepan over medium high heat. Add the sausage and cook, stirring constantly, until lightly browned, 5 to 8 minutes. Remove the sausage from the pan and drain off any fat. Heat the remaining 4 tablespoons oil in the pan and add the onions, carrots, celery, and garlic. Sauté over medium high heat for 10 minutes. Add the tomatoes, basil, parsley, and red pepper. Cook, uncovered, at a slow boil for about 30 minutes. Season with salt and pepper. Serve over hot pasta (fusilli, penne, or ziti is recommended). Pass grated Parmesan cheese at the table.

Sun-Dried Tomato Sauce

The almonds give this rich uncooked sauce an interesting texture while the sun-dried tomatoes yield a mellow, sweet flavor. Like a stew, the sauce tastes even better then second day. This superb sauce will keep in the refrigerator for 2 to 3 weeks and it also freezes well.

If you have sun-dried tomatoes that are packed in oil, skip the step that calls for soaking the tomatoes in hot water.

2 cups sun-dried tomatoes
2 cups hot water
1 garlic clove
1 small onion
¼ cup olive oil
¼ cup soybean or other vegetable oil
⅓ cup fresh lemon juice
¼ cup freshly grated Parmesan cheese
⅓ cup slivered almonds, chopped

1 teaspoon dried basil
¼ teaspoon dried thyme
¼ teaspoon dried savory
½ teaspoon dried oregano
Salt and freshly ground pepper to taste

Yield: 4 servings

Combine the tomatoes and hot water and set aside for 5 minutes to allow the tomatoes to soften. Drain and reserve 1½ cups of the water.

In a food processor fitted with a steel blade, chop the garlic and onion. Add the tomatoes and process carefully by pulsing the machine on and off until the tomatoes are just chopped. Do not overprocess or you will wind up with a paste.

Add the oils, lemon juice, Parmesan cheese, almonds, herbs, and salt and pepper. Process *very* briefly, just to mix in, still preserving the rough texture. Pour the sauce into a bowl and stir in enough of the reserved tomato soaking water to make a loose, but chunky tomato sauce. Set aside for at least 30 minutes to allow the flavors to blend. Taste and adjust the seasonings. Serve over hot pasta.

Fresh Tomato and Broccoli Sauce

Tomato and broccoli may make an unlikely combination, but the intense flavor of the sauce proves the match works.

4 tablespoons olive oil
2 garlic cloves, minced
1 cup chopped onions
1 teaspoon crushed dried red hot pepper flakes
8 medium-sized tomatoes, peeled, seeded, and chopped
2 tablespoons chopped anchovies
Salt and pepper to taste
2 cups broccoli florets
Grated Parmesan cheese
¼ cup pine nuts

Yield: 4 servings

Heat 2 tablespoons of the oil in a saucepan over medium heat. Add 1 garlic clove, ½ cup of the onions, and the red pepper. Sauté for 3 minutes. Add the tomatoes and anchovies. Season with salt and pepper. Bring to a boil, then reduce the heat to low, and cook for 15 minutes.

While the tomato sauce cooks, heat the remaining 2 tablespoons olive oil in a medium-size skillet. Add the remaining ½ cup onions and 1 garlic clove. Sauté for 3 minutes over medium heat. Add the broccoli and sauté until the broccoli is bright green and just tender. Add to the tomato sauce. Mix gently and keep the sauce hot over low heat.

Serve over hot pasta (farfelle or ziti is recommended) and sprinkle with cheese and pine nuts. Serve immediately.

Eggplant Sauté

The cumin, olives, and feta cheese provide a Middle Eastern flair for this vegetarian sauce.

¼ cup olive oil
2 tablespoons cumin
3 garlic cloves, minced
1½ pounds eggplant
1 (28-ounce) can peeled tomatoes, drained (reserving the juice) and chopped
1 green pepper, diced
1 red pepper, diced
Salt and pepper to taste
1 teaspoon hot pepper sauce (not Tabasco)
20 to 25 pitted Greek black olives
½ pound crumbled feta cheese

Yield: 4 to 5 servings

Heat the oil in a large skillet. Add the cumin, garlic, and eggplant and cook until the eggplant is soft, about 10 minutes, adding the juice from the tomatoes to prevent burning. Add the green and red peppers and sauté until they begin to soften, 2 to 3 minutes. Stir in the tomatoes. Taste and add salt and pepper. Cover and simmer for 10 to 20 minutes.

Serve over hot pasta (mostaccioli, ziti, or penne is recommended). Top with the feta cheese. Toss gently and serve at once.

Spicy Vegetable Sauce

In the mood for something light and fresh? Try a peppery blend of vegetables.

2 tablespoons olive oil
2 tablespoons butter
1 cup julienned carrots
1 cup julienned onions
1 garlic clove, minced
1 cup julienned zucchini
1 cup julienned yellow squash
¼ teaspoon white pepper
¼ teaspoon cayenne pepper
½ teaspoon paprika
½ teaspoon black pepper
½ teaspoon dried oregano
2 tablespoons flour
⅔ cup dry white wine
½ cup water

Juice of 1 lemon
2 medium-size fresh Italian plum tomatoes, halved and sliced

Yield: 4 servings

Heat the oil and butter in a large saucepan over medium heat. Add the carrots, onions, and garlic and sauté for 3 minutes. Add the zucchini, yellow squash, and spices. Continue to sauté for 3 minutes. Reduce the heat to medium low and stir in the flour, blending it into the vegetables. Slowly add the wine and water, stirring constantly until the sauce has thickened. Add the lemon juice and tomatoes. Slowly cook for 5 more minutes. Serve over hot pasta (spinach fusilli or penne is recommended).

Note: To julienne squash, cut slices of squash with skin $1/_8$ inch thick. Cut these slices into strips $1/_8$ inch thick and 2 inches long. Use only those strips that have skin on one surface.

Pesto Vegetable Sauce

Another flavorful vegetarian sauce, this one derives its flavor from basil.

2 tablespoons olive oil
1 large onion, coarsely chopped
1 green pepper, cubed (1-inch pieces)
6 large mushrooms, sliced
1 garlic clove, minced
½ pound cherry tomatoes, halved
¼ cup chopped fresh parsley
½ cup chopped black olives
½ cup fresh lemon juice
¼ cup dry red wine
2 tablespoons Classic Basil Pesto (page 27)

Heat the oil over medium high heat in a large saucepan. Add the onion, green pepper, mushrooms, and garlic. Sauté for 5 minutes, or until the vegetables are just tender. Add the remaining ingredients and stir until well blended. Cook, partially covered, for 10 minutes. Serve over hot pasta (a short pasta, such as ziti, penne, fusilli, or farfelle is recommended). Pass grated cheese on the side.

Yield: 4 to 6 servings

Artichoke and Caper Sauce

Capers are the green flower buds of a perennial shrub found in Southern Europe. These sharp-tasting little pickles are a perfect foil for the mellow flavor of the artichokes.

2 tablespoons butter
2 tablespoons olive oil
2 medium-size onions, chopped
2 garlic cloves, crushed
3 tablespoons all-purpose flour
1 cup chicken broth or chicken stock
¾ cup dry white wine
1½ cups peeled, seeded, and chopped ripe tomatoes or 1 (1-pound) can Italian tomatoes, drained and sliced
1 (14-ounce) can artichoke hearts packed in water, drained
2 teaspoons dried or 2 tablespoons chopped fresh basil
2 tablespoons capers
Salt and pepper to taste

Yield: 4 to 6 servings

In a medium-size skillet, heat the butter and oil over medium heat. Add the onions and garlic and sauté until pale gold. Stir in the flour and cook gently until well blended. Add the chicken broth and wine, stirring constantly until the sauce is thickened. Add the tomatoes and artichokes and stir into the sauce. Reduce the heat to a simmer and add the basil and capers. Season with salt and pepper. Simmer for another 3 to 5 minutes to allow the flavors to blend.

Serve over hot pasta (fusilli or tagliatelli is recommended) and sprinkle with grated Parmesan cheese.

Chicken Artichoke Sauce

3 tablespoons olive oil
1 pound chicken breast, skin removed
   and cut into strips
½ cup chopped shallots
2 tablespoons flour
1-½ cups chicken broth or stock
1 cup dry white wine
2 tablespoons capers, drained
1 tablespoon lemon juice
¼ teaspoon black pepper
1 (14-ounce) can artichoke hearts,
   drained and cut into quarters
¼ pound snowpeas, cut into thin slivers

Yield: 4 to 6 servings

In a medium-size skillet, heat the oil over medium-high heat. Add the chicken and sauté until the chicken is lightly brown. Reduce the heat to medium-low and add the shallots. Sauté for 2 minutes. Sprinkle the flour over the chicken and shallots, stirring constantly until the flour is well blended. Add the chicken broth and wine. Cook, stirring, until the sauce has thickened. Add the capers, lemon juice, pepper, artichokes, and snowpeas and cook for about 3 minutes. Serve over hot pasta.

Lemony Chicken Zucchini Sauce

A light, zesty sauce with colorful flecks of green from the zucchini.

¼ cup olive oil
5 large garlic cloves, minced
2 whole boneless chicken breast, cut into
  2-inch strips
2½ tablespoons flour
1 cup dry white wine
1 cup chicken broth
Juice of 1 lemon
1 cup coarsely grated zucchini, firmly
  packed
4 scallions, including green tops, sliced
¼ teaspoon black pepper
1 teaspoon dried summer savory
Salt to taste

Yield: 4 servings

Heat the oil in a large skillet over medium high heat. Add the garlic and chicken and sauté for 4 minutes. Sprinkle the flour over the chicken and mix well. Reduce the heat to medium and add the wine, chicken stock, and lemon juice. Cook, stirring constantly, until the sauce thickens. Stir in the zucchini, scallions, black pepper, and summer savory and heat through. Season with salt. Serve over hot pasta (linguine is recommended).

Cajun Chicken-Sweet Pepper Sauce

A sweet sauce enhanced by the punch of Cajun spices. To simplify the recipe, you can use a commercial blend of Cajun spices, such as Paul Prudhomme's Louisiana Cajun Vegetable Magic or Chicken Magic instead of making up your own seasoning mix.

Cajun Seasoning Mix

½ teaspoon salt
½ teaspoon white pepper
½ teaspoon cayenne pepper
½ teaspoon black pepper
½ teaspoon dried basil
¼ teaspoon dried thyme

Sauce

3 tablespoons olive oil
1 tablespoon butter

1 to 1¼ pounds boned and skinned chicken breast, cut into slices about ¼ inch wide
½ cup chopped onions
2½ cups chicken stock or broth
1 small green pepper, julienned
1 small sweet red pepper, julienned
1 small sweet yellow pepper, julienned
½ cup sliced scallions, including some greens
1½ tablespoons arrowroot or 2 tablespoons cornstarch

Yield: 4 to 6 servings

Combine the Cajun seasonings and set aside. Heat the oil and butter in large saucepan over medium-high heat. Add the chicken and sauté until lightly browned, about 5 minutes. Remove the saucepan from the heat and add the Cajun seasonings. Blend into the chicken.

Return the saucepan to medium heat and add the onions. Sauté for 2 minutes. Add the chicken stock or broth and cook for 2 minutes.

Combine the arrowroot or cornstarch with just enough cold water to make a thick paste. Add to the sauce and stir constantly until the sauce thickens. Add the peppers and scallions and simmer for 5 minutes.

Serve over hot pasta (thick spaghetti broken into thirds before it is cooked is recommended).

Prosciutto and Basil Sauce

Prosciutto is a lightly salted, air-cured ham, the best of which comes from Parma. Prosciutto di Parma is made from pigs richly nourished from the whey that is the by-product of making Parmesan cheese.

2 tablespoons butter
2 tablespoons olive oil
¼ pound prosciutto, sliced into
   matchsticks
1 onion, chopped
2 garlic cloves, minced
1 (28-ounce) can Italian plum tomatoes,
   drained
¼ cup chopped fresh parsley
½ cup chopped fresh basil
½ cup dry red wine

Yield: 4 servings

Heat the butter and oil over medium heat in a skillet. Add the prosciutto and sauté until lightly browned, about 3 minutes. Add the onion and garlic and sauté for about 2 minutes. Reduce the heat and add the tomatoes, parsley, basil, and wine. Cook, uncovered, for 15 to 20 minutes.

Serve over hot pasta (spaghetti is recommended) and pass grated Parmesan cheese on the side.

Mixed Pepper-Sausage Sauce

½ pound sweet Italian sausages
2 tablespoons olive oil
1 cup chopped onions
1 cup green pepper strips (1½ inches by ½ inch)
1 cup sweet yellow pepper strips (1½ long by ½ inch)
1 cup sweet red pepper strips (1½ inches by ½ inch)
Salt and freshly ground black pepper to taste
1 cup whipping cream or half-and-half

Yield: 4 servings

Remove the casings and break up the sausage meat into small pieces. In a large skillet, brown the sausage over medium heat, stirring occasionally and breaking up the meat into small pieces. Drain and set aside.

In a medium-sized sauté pan, heat the oil and butter over medium heat. Add the onions and sauté until the onions are golden, about 5 minutes. Add the peppers and sauté until just tender, 3 to 4 minutes; don't overcook. Season with salt and pepper. Stir in the cream and continue to cook for about 4 minutes. Remove from the heat and add the sausage. Serve immediately over hot pasta (rotelle or conchiglie is recommended).

Black Bean Sauce

Black beans pair well with smoked sausages. Here's a hearty sauce, slowly cooked and highly seasoned—good for a cold winter's night. Serve with plenty of beer.

1 cup dry black beans
3 tablespoons olive oil
1 cup chopped onions
3 garlic cloves, crushed
1 carrot, grated
¼ teaspoon crushed dried red pepper flakes
½ teaspoon freshly ground black pepper
1 teaspoon whole cumin seeds
Salt to taste
1 cup freshly chopped tomatoes
3 cups water
Juice of 1 lemon juice

½ pound smoked sausage (kielbasa or chorizo), cubed
Sour cream

Yield: 4 servings

Soak the beans in cold water to cover for 4 to 6 hours.

In a medium-size saucepan, heat the oil. Add the onions, garlic, and carrot and sauté over medium heat until golden, about 5 minutes. Add the red pepper, black pepper, cumin seeds, and salt. Drain the black beans and add, along with the tomatoes and 3 cups of water. Bring to a boil, then reduce the heat to low, and cook, partially covered, until the beans are tender, about 2 hours. Remove from the heat and add the lemon juice.

Puree about 1½ cups of the sauce in a food processor or blender. Return to the saucepan along with the sausage. Cook for another 15 minutes over low heat.

Serve over hot pasta (farfelle is recommended) and top each serving with a dollop of sour cream.

Yellow Tomato Sauce with Cilantro

Yellow tomatoes are very delicately flavored, allowing the tastes of other ingredients to emerge in a sauce. They pair nicely with cilantro, which has a distinctively sharp, smoky flavor.

¼ cup olive oil
½ cup thinly sliced scallions, including
    some green tops
1 celery rib, finely chopped
1¾ pounds yellow tomatoes, peeled and
    chopped
Salt and pepper to taste
1 medium-size sweet red pepper,
    chopped
½ cup chopped fresh cilantro
Juice of 1 lemon

Yield: 4 servings

Heat the oil in a skillet over medium heat and add half the scallions and the celery. Sauté for 3 minutes. Add the tomatoes and season with salt and pepper. Bring the mixture to a slow boil and cook for 10 minutes. Add the red pepper, cilantro, lemon juice, and remaining scallions. Cook, uncovered, for about 10 minutes, or until the sauce has slightly thickened. Serve over hot pasta (fusilli or penne is recommended).

6
Ten Minute Sauces

Creamy Tomato Sauce

Here's a rich, flavorful sauce to make when you want a quick sauce to serve over fresh or frozen ravioli.

4 tablespoons butter
½ cup chopped onion
1 small garlic clove, minced
2 cups canned crushed tomatoes
1 teaspoon dried marjoram
1¼ cups whipping cream

Yield: 4 servings

In a saucepan over medium heat, melt the butter. Add the onion and garlic and sauté until the onion is pale gold, about 5 minutes. Add the tomatoes and marjoram. Stir to blend. Add the cream and heat until hot and bubbly, stirring constantly. Serve over hot pasta and pass freshly grated Parmesan cheese on the side.

Arugula and Fresh Tomato Sauce

Arugula is a green that goes by several names, including rocket and raquette. Its peppery taste blends well with tomatoes. The young leaves are also good in salads when combined with lettuce and other mild-flavored greens.

¼ cup olive oil
2 garlic cloves, minced
2 pounds fresh tomatoes, peeled, seeded, and chopped
2 cups chopped arugula
2 scallions, sliced
1½ cups grated Parmesan cheese

Yield: 4 servings

Heat the oil in a large skillet over medium heat. Add the garlic and cook until golden and fragrant, about 3 minutes. Add the tomatoes and cook, stirring constantly, for about 4 minutes. Add the arugula and scallions and cook for 1 minute more.

Serve over hot pasta (penne is recommended). Top with the cheese and serve.

Pistachio Pesto

Pistachio pesto is an interesting variation on the classic pesto (page 27), which is made with pine nuts or walnuts.

2 cups fresh basil leaves
2 large garlic cloves
¼ cup freshly grated Parmesan cheese
⅓ cup shelled unsalted pistachio nuts
½ cup olive oil
Salt and freshly ground pepper to taste

Yield: 4 to 6 servings

Combine the basil, garlic, cheese, and pistachio nuts in a food processor or blender. Process to mix. With the machine running, slowly add the olive oil. Season with salt and pepper and process to the desired consistency. Let stand for 5 minutes.

To serve, thin the pesto with a few tablespoons of hot pasta cooking water and toss with hot pasta (fettuccine or linguine is recommended).

Winter Kale Pesto

Kale, dried basil, and sunflower seeds make up this unusual dark green pesto, perfect for making in the winter when fresh basil is not available.

1 cup chopped fresh kale, stems removed
½ cup dried basil
2 medium-size garlic cloves
2 tablespoons freshly grated Parmesan cheese
¼ cup sunflower seeds
¾ cup olive oil
Salt and freshly ground pepper to taste

Yield: 4 to 6 servings

Combine the kale, basil, garlic, cheese, and sunflower seeds in a blender. Process to mix. With the blender running, slowly add the olive oil. Season with salt and pepper. Process to the desired consistency.

To serve, thin the pesto with a few tablespoons of hot pasta cooking water and toss with hot pasta (a whole wheat pasta is recommended).

Pesto Tomato Sauce

This sauce is whipped together in a blender or food processor, then heated briefly. There is no oil in the sauce, which should appeal to those watching their diets.

1½ cups crushed canned tomatoes or
   tomato puree
2 cups fresh spinach leaves, packed
1 cup Italian parsley leaves, packed
½ cup fresh basil leaves
2 garlic cloves
½ cup grated Parmesan cheese
Juice of 1 lemon
¼ cup walnuts

Yield: 4 to 6 servings

Combine all the ingredients in a blender or food processor and blend until you have a coarsely textured sauce. Pour into a saucepan and heat over medium heat, stirring constantly, until hot. Toss with hot pasta and sprinkle with additional Parmesan cheese. Serve immediately.

Zucchini-Mushroom Sauce

Mushroom powder, available at gourmet food shops, gives the sauce a pungent flavor, while the Canadian bacon adds a slightly smoky undertone. The combination produces a very full-flavored sauce.

3 tablespoons butter
½ pound mushrooms, sliced
3 scallions, including some green tops, thinly sliced
4 (¼-inch-thick) slices Canadian bacon, cut into thin strips
2 cups coarsely grated raw zucchini, packed
2 tablespoons flour
2 tablespoons mushroom powder
1 teaspoon dried rosemary
1 cup water
1 cup dry white wine

Yield: 4 to 6 servings

Melt the butter in a large skillet over medium high heat. Add the sliced mushrooms and sauté for 4 minutes. Add the scallions, Canadian bacon, and zucchini and sauté for 3 minutes. Sprinkle the flour and mushroom powder over the mixture, stirring until well blended. Add the rosemary, water, and wine, stirring constantly, and cook until the sauce has thickened, 3 to 4 minutes. Serve over hot pasta (fettuccine or tagliatelli is recommended). Pass freshly grated Parmesan cheese at the table.

Garden Sauce with Fresh Herbs

2 to 3 medium-size sweet red peppers
2 tablespoons olive or other vegetable oil
1 tablespoon butter
¼ cup chopped garlic
1 cup chopped onion
⅔ cup very finely diced carrots
2 cups chopped mushrooms
¼ cup minced fresh herbs (a combination of thyme, savory, oregano is recommended)
½ cup chicken stock or broth
⅓ cup chopped fresh parsley
Salt and freshly ground pepper to taste

Yield: 4 servings

Roast the red peppers on a long-handled fork over a gas or electric burner on high. Hold the peppers close to the heat, turning as they char and blister. Place in a paper bag, close the top, and allow the peppers to steam for about 10 minutes. Loosen and remove the skins. Peel the stem away, removing the seeds and veins. Roughly chop the peppers. You should have 1 cup chopped roasted red peppers.

Heat the oil and butter in a large skillet and add the garlic, onion, and carrots. Sauté until the vegetables are softened, 2 to 3 minutes. Add the chopped red peppers, mushrooms, herbs, and chicken stock. Simmer gently, stirring frequently, until the sauce has reduced by half. Fold in the parsley. Season with salt and pepper.

Serve over hot pasta (fresh tomato linguine is recommended). Pass freshly grated Parmesan cheese on the side.

Broccoli Blue Cheese Sauce

1 cup chicken stock or broth
6 cups chopped broccoli stems and
   florets
3 cups chopped zucchini
1¼ cups crumbled blue cheese
Freshly ground pepper to taste

Yield: 4 to 6 servings

In a medium-size saucepan, heat the chicken stock to boiling. Add the broccoli and zucchini. Cover, reduce the heat, and simmer, until just tender, 4 to 5 minutes. Pour into a bowl and add the cheese and pepper.

Serve over hot pasta (fresh or dried linguine or fresh Chinese wheat noodles is recommended).

Broccoli de Rabe and Garlic Sauce

Broccoli de rabe is a tender, mild green frequently found in Italian cooking. It is often described as a cross between broccoli and mustard greens. The leaves are shaped like turnip greens, and most stems contain small bud clusters, like miniature broccoli heads.

6 cups loosely packed, coarsely chopped broccoli de rabe
2 tablespoons olive oil
1 tablespoon minced garlic
1 tablespoon crushed dried red pepper flakes
1½ tablespoons pine nuts (optional)
Salt and freshly ground pepper to taste

Yield: 3 to 4 servings

Steam or blanch the broccoli de rabe in at least 3 quarts of boiling salted water until just tender, about 5 minutes. Drain well.

In a large skillet, heat the oil. Add the garlic, red pepper, and pine nuts and sauté for 2 minutes. Add the blanched greens and sauté for 2 to 3 minutes, until very tender. Season with salt and pepper. Serve over hot pasta (fresh or dried tomato linguine or fettuccine is recommended). Pass freshly grated Parmesan cheese on the side.

Index

THE CROSSING PRESS
publishes a full line of cookbooks.
For a free catalog, call toll-free

800 / 777-1048

Please specify a *cookbook* catalog.